REH ★ PRO LESSONS

INTERVALLIC DESIGNS for Jazz Guitar

Audio Assets Included

by

Joe Diorio

T0045630

PLAYBACK+
Speed · Pitch · Balance · Loop

To access audio visit:
www.halleonard.com/mylibrary

Enter Code
7491-8304-5486-4334

Dedicated to Wally Cirillo
A very special thanks to Don Mock for his encouragement

ISBN 978-0-634-02006-3

HAL•LEONARD® CORPORATION
7777 W. BLUEMOUND RD. P.O. BOX 13819 MILWAUKEE, WI 53213

Visit Hal Leonard Online at
www.halleonard.com

Table of Contents

Introduction

To help you understand the music in this book and use it to its full potential, I'd like to give you a general idea of my concept of music. A little over twenty years ago, due to the many years that I'd already been playing guitar and the varied experiences I'd had, I arrived at a point in my musical life where diatonic harmony, chord symbols, key signatures, key centers, or similar devices no longer had any hold on me. In short, I became liberated—freed from the weight of *thinking* of music as opposed to just *playing* it. Bear in mind, this took 28 years.

All the designs in this book were conceived at this point of departure from diatonic music. They came out of my intuitive sense and not from a mechanical formula. I wrote them down as they were being born. Gradually, I began to realize how to use them in other situations aside from freestyle playing. I started to incorporate them into tunes with chord changes, and found a way to sound "inside" and "outside" at the same time.

I began to see the two-fold nature of these ideas: that they waver in and out of tonality and are perfect for both tonal and atonal playing. For many of these designs, I have made chord suggestions to give them a bit of harmonic stability. And I'm sure you will find many more chords with which they will fit. But I caution you not to limit them to chords alone, for they are also very powerful under free circumstances.

Let me offer this advice:

1. Practice these lines *very* slowly, at least a dozen times or more. In this way, the mind will record the music correctly. Playing fast leads to many mistakes, which later must be reprogrammed.
2. The interval skips may be new to some of you, and learning to play them will be difficult. They will, however, increase your technical ability, which of course will lead to greater freedom. So be patient.
3. The first finger always determines the position you are in.
4. Transpose all these lines to other keys when range will allow.

It's important to leave your mind open for new sounds, especially those of the modern composers and players. This will help expand your hearing ability and widen your imagination. You may want to experiment by using parts of a design, or combining different lines. All in all, it's a matter of keeping your eyes and ears open for the sounds you want. Remember that each person grows at their own rate, and that rushing only leads to frustration, so relax and enjoy music!

Designs of Tonality

The A minor pentatonic scale (spelled A–C–D–E–G) is the general sound of the first ten designs. The B note is added to several of the lines to increase melodic strength. These pentatonic designs are adaptable and colorful for all styles of improvising.

Once the material is fully digested and the ear has become familiar with the sounds of these designs, the intuitive sense will take over and you will have the freedom to play them under tonal or atonal circumstances. There are many other chords related to these lines aside from the ones I suggest; this area is very flexible. Also remember that the suggested fingerings and picking technique (alternating down, up) may be changed to each player's preference. Try each of the first ten designs over: Am11, Asus4, Dm9, Em11, and Fmaj7. The numbers between the staff and tablature are the suggested left-hand fingerings.

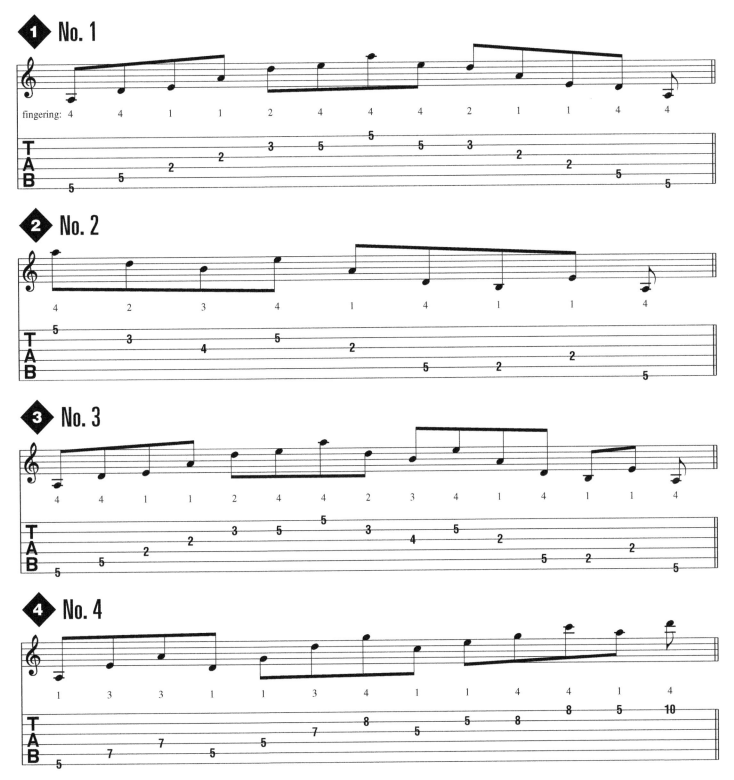

No. 5

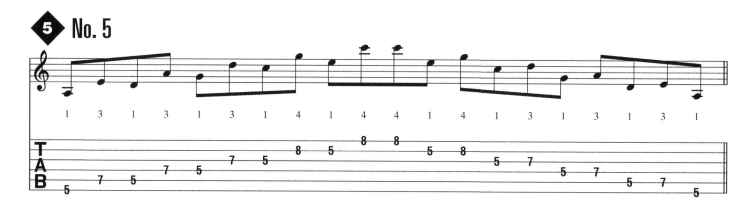

No. 6

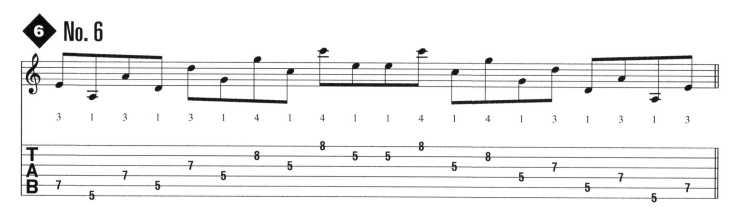

No. 7

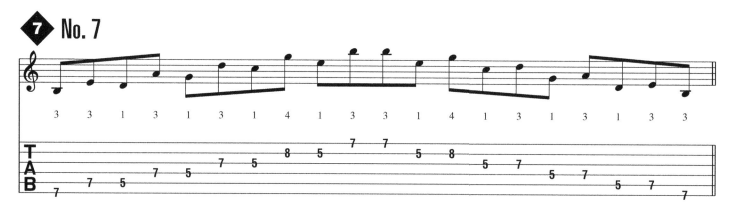

No. 8

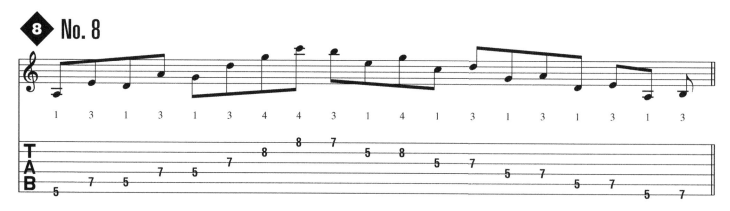

No. 9

10 No. 10

Try these next three designs over C7, C9, C13, Gm6, Gm7, Gm9, Em7♭5, or B♭maj7♭5.

11 No. 11

* Note: Accidentals apply to assigned notes only.

12 No. 12

13 No. 13

This design works over B♭m7, B♭m9, B♭m13, B♭m11, D♭maj7♭5, D♭maj9♭5, or D♭maj13♭5.

14 No. 14

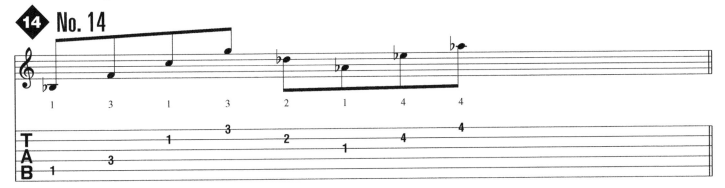

7

This one works over C7 and alterations, F#7, F#9, F#13, G#6, C#m7, C#m9, A#m7♭5, or Emaj7♭5.

15 No. 15

Once again, try this design over C7 and alterations.

16 No. 16

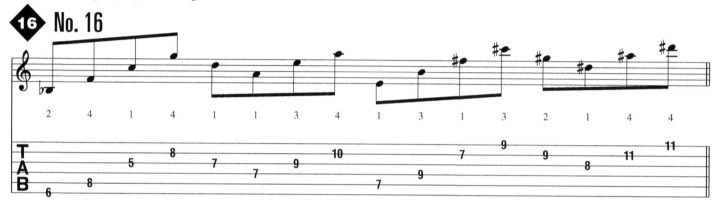

Try this last one over B♭7 and alterations.

17 No. 17

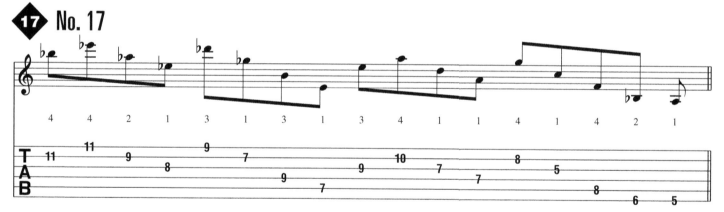

Designs of Diatonic Harmonies

These designs apply to any given chord in the key of D major. For example, when thinking harmonically, if you see A13, any of these lines will work well for that chord. Once again, however, realize that you do not need to restrict yourself to the key.

The diatonic chords in D major are: Dmaj7, Em7, F#m7, Gmaj7, A7, Bm7, and C#m7♭5.

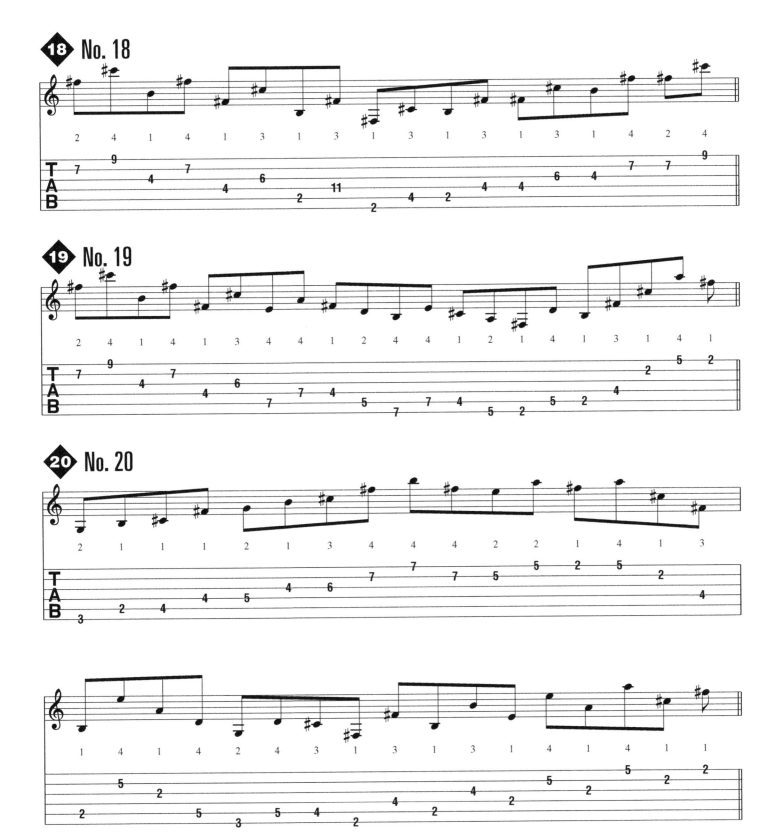

21 **No. 21**

22 **No. 22**

23 **No. 23**

No. 24 has a free tonality about it that works well with or without harmonic stability.

24 **No. 24**

Designs for the Diminished Scales

There are only three diminished scales. They are C dim, Db dim, and D dim. The construction of each scale is the same: alternating whole steps and half steps. Here is the C diminished scale:
Notice that by using the notes C, Eb, Gb, or A (which are all a minor third apart) as starting points, we have

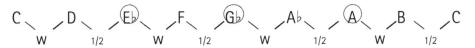

the C diminished scale starting on different pitches. Therefore, the C diminished scale provides us with three other diminished scales: Eb dim, Gb dim, and A dim. Similarly, the Db diminished scale will yield Db dim, E dim, G dim, and Bb dim scales. The D diminished scale gives us D dim, F dim, Ab dim, and B dim scales. This covers all 12 possibilities for the diminished scale.

Now let us examine the four dominant seventh chords related to the C diminished scale: B7, D7, F7, and Ab7. The C diminished scale against any of these dominant seventh chords produces the following chordal tones: 1, 3, 5, b7, b9, #9, #11 or b5, and 13. At this point, we can see the flexibility of this scale when we deal with the alterations of the seventh chord (e.g., B7b5, B7b9, B7#9, B7b5b9, B7b5b9#9).

The diminished scale generally begins a half step above the root of the dominant chord. For example, if B7 were the dominant chord, we would use the C diminished scale, which is a half step above B. Another way of looking at this is to start on the tonic note of the dominant chord and build the diminished scale starting with a half step. This would look as follows:

Remember that you are actually playing the C diminished scale starting on B, not the B diminished scale.

$$B \diagdown_{1/2} \diagup C \diagdown_{} \diagup_{W} D \diagdown_{1/2} \diagup Eb \diagdown_{} \diagup_{W} F \diagdown_{1/2} \diagup Gb \diagdown_{} \diagup_{W} Ab \diagdown_{1/2} \diagup A \diagdown_{} \diagup_{W} B$$

Keep in mind also that each design may be transposed up or down in minor thirds, and applied to the same chord, enabling us to include the entire range of the guitar. By transposing one design in minor thirds (e.g., C to Eb to Gb to A), you can complete the minor third cycle and take control of the seventh chord and its alterations.

Here's a chart for finding the diminished scale for its given seventh chords:

Dominant 7th Chord

B7	D7	F7	Ab7	C7	Eb7	Gb7	A7	Db7	E7	G7	Bb7
C	Eb	Gb	A	Db	E	G	Bb	D	F	Ab	B

Diminished Scale

There are other functions for the diminished scale. For minor chords (m6, m7, m7b5), start on the root of the minor chord (e.g., for Cm7, play C dim scale starting on the root C). And of course, the most obvious use for the diminished scale is over the diminished seventh chord, which starts on the root (e.g., for C°7, play C dim scale).

Designs 25 through 27 are intended to work over the dominant chords G7, Bb7, Db7, E7, and all of their alterations.

25 ## No. 25

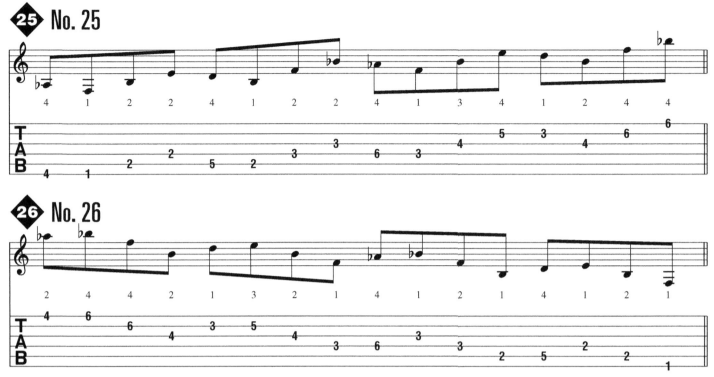

26 ## No. 26

No. 27 is an F diminished design of major 7ths moving up by minor 3rds. I think of no. 28 as an Ab diminished design.

27 ## No. 27

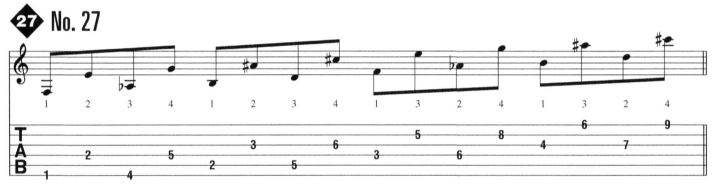

28 ## No. 28

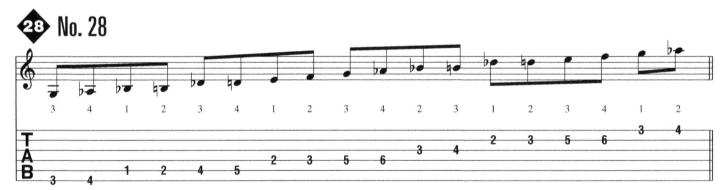

29 ## No. 29

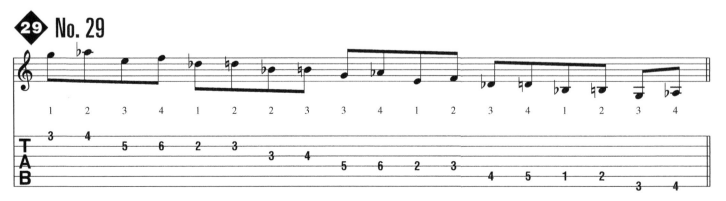

Combinations of D, F, A♭, and B Diminished Designs 25 through 29
(for E7, G7, B♭7, D♭7, and their alterations)

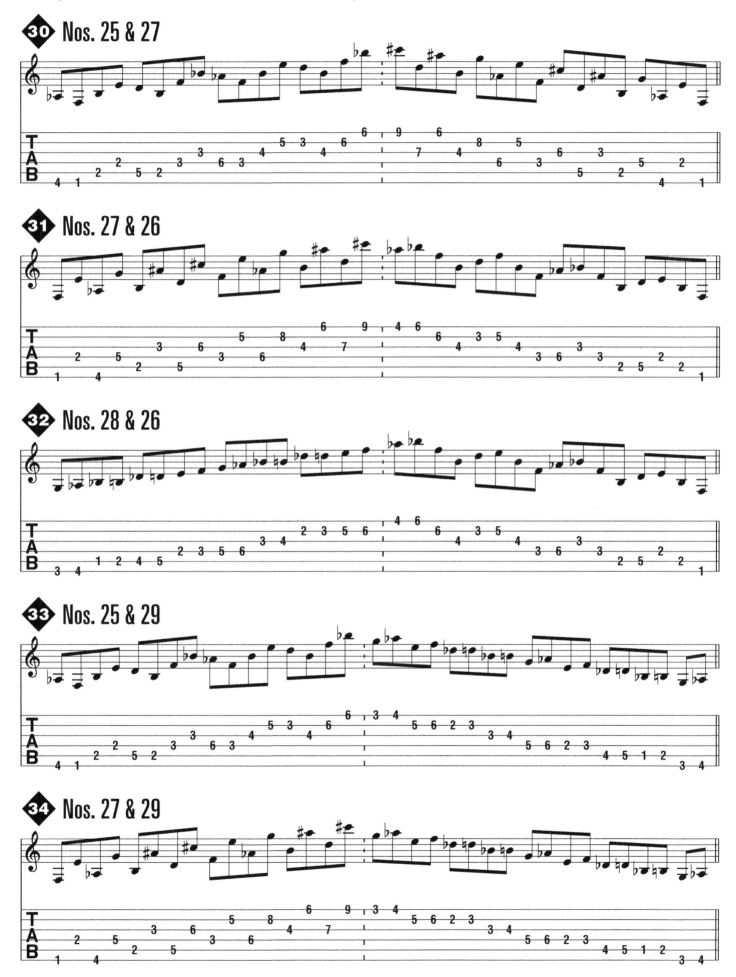

35 ◈ Nos. 28 & 27

The G7♭5 arpeggio is inserted here and combined with the already explained diminished lines. The insertion of this arpeggio does not limit us to only G7♭5. By examining the relationship of the notes in G7♭5 to the other three dominant chords (B♭7, D♭7, and E7), the following alterations occur:

	G	B	D♭	F
G7♭5	1	3	♭5	♭7
B♭7	13	♭9	#9	5
D♭7	♭5	♭7	1	3
E7	#9	5	13	♭9

36 ◈ No. 30

G7♭5

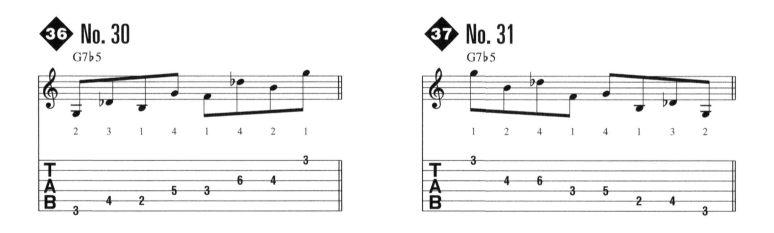

37 ◈ No. 31

G7♭5

38 ◈ Nos. 30 & 29

39 Nos. 28 & 31

40 Nos. 30 & 26

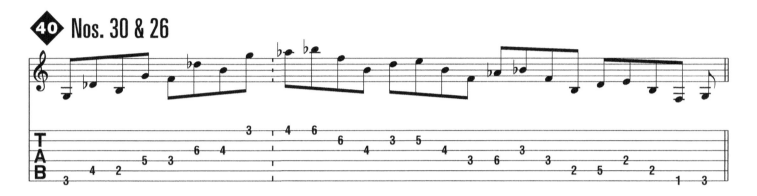

41 Nos. 25 & 31

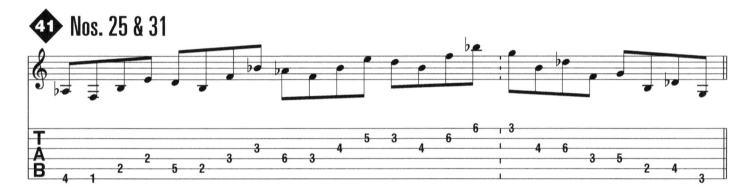

42 Nos. 27 & 31

43 Nos. 30 & 27

Designs for Dominant and Altered Dominant Chords

This chapter continues with more lines dealing with the dominant seventh chord. Here, I base all the designs on A7 and its alterations. Some suggestions are: A7♭5, A7♭9, A7♭5♭9, A7♯9, A13♭5, A13♭5♭9, and A7♭5♭9♯5. These designs should be transposed to all other dominant chords.

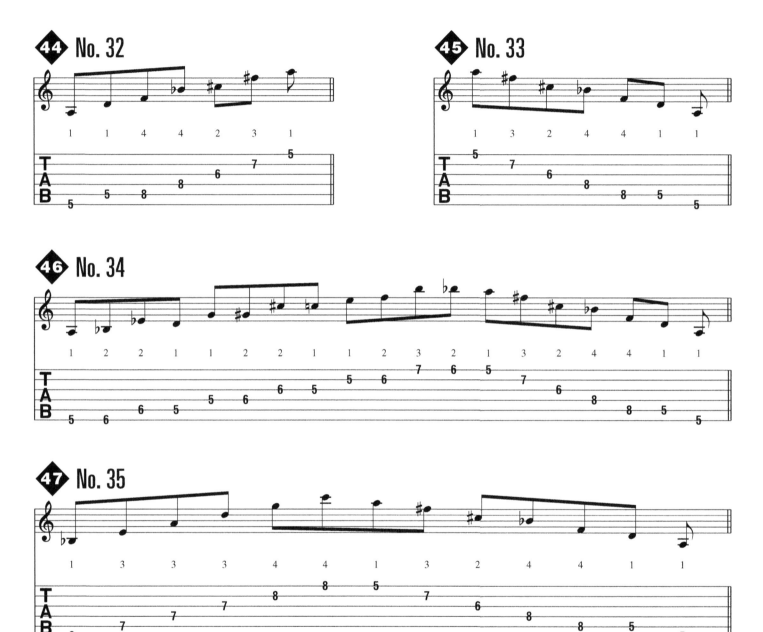

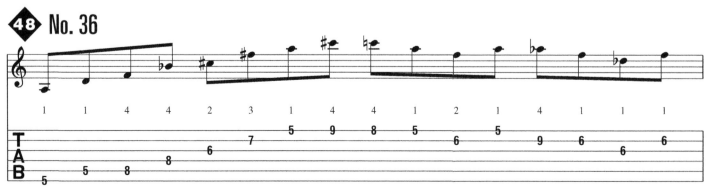

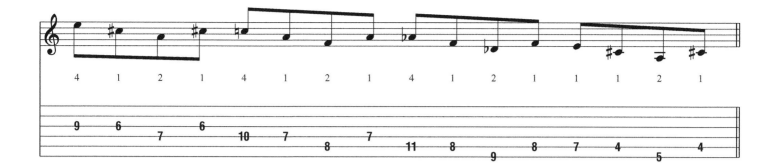

49 No. 37

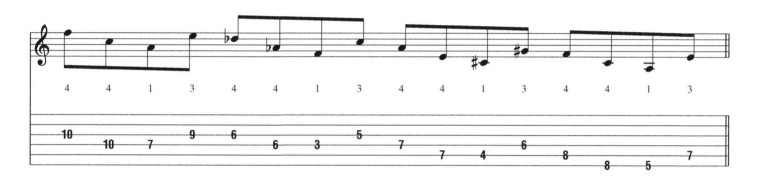

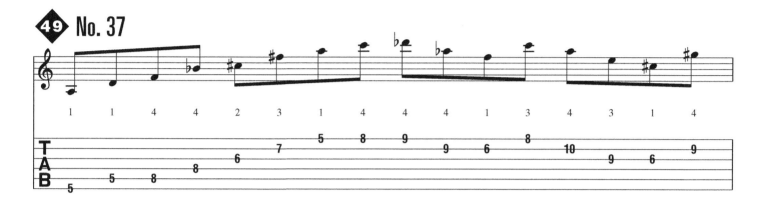

50 No. 38

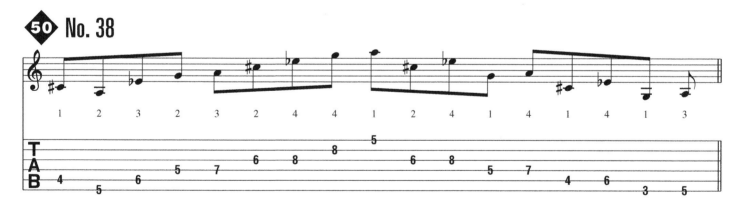

51 No. 39

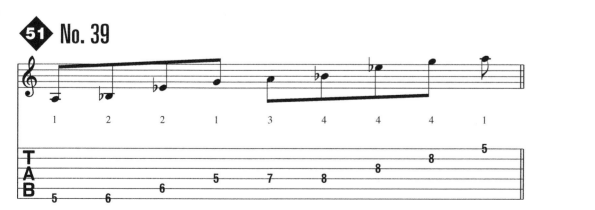

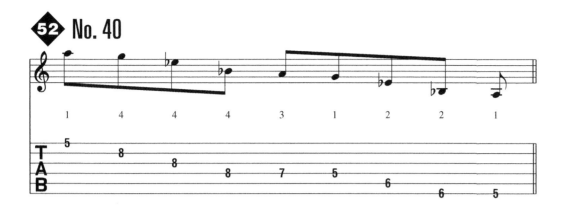

53 Nos. 39 & 38

54 Nos. 38 & 40

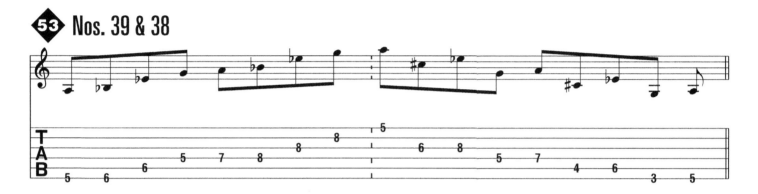

55 No. 41

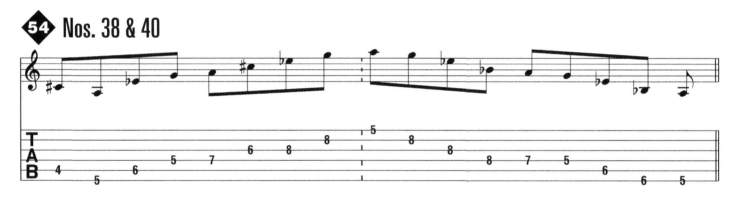

56 Nos. 41 & 40

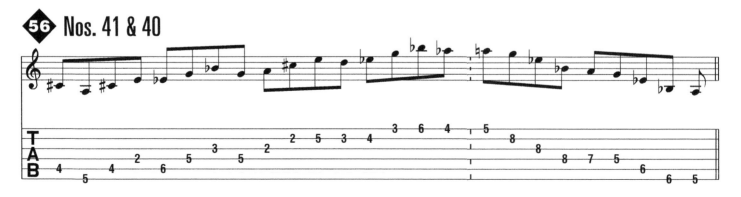

Designs for the Chromatic Scales

This chapter begins with two chromatic scales. When used by themselves, they fit any chord type—major, minor, or dominant and their alterations—simply because the chromatic scale contains every note of every chord.

57 No. 42

C chromatic scale in fourths

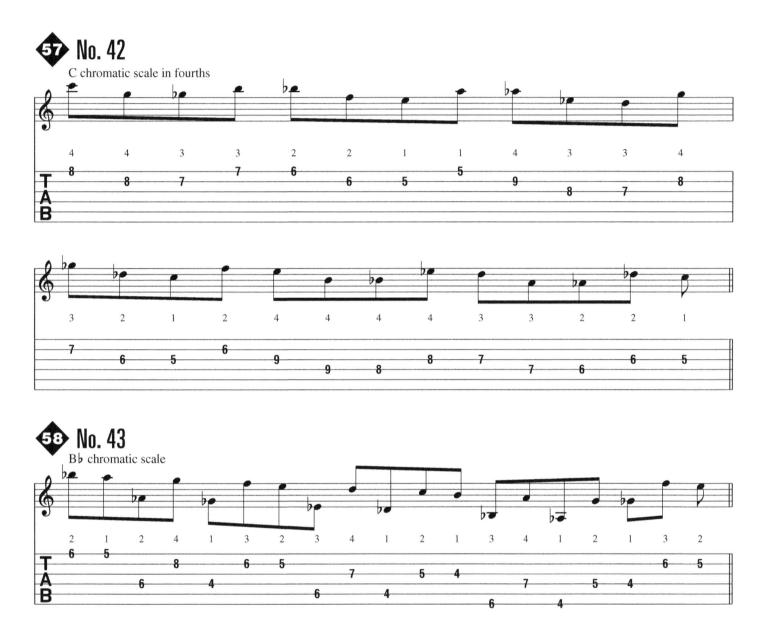

58 No. 43

Bb chromatic scale

By joining the previous chromatic scales with designs 44 and 45, we have four designs for the suggested chords of C9, Gm6, Em7b5, and Bbmaj7b5. (Note that Gm6 and Em7b5 are the same chord, and C9 is the same as Gm6 and Em7b5 without the root C.)

59 No. 44

Gm6, Em7b5, Bbmaj7b5, or C9 and extensions

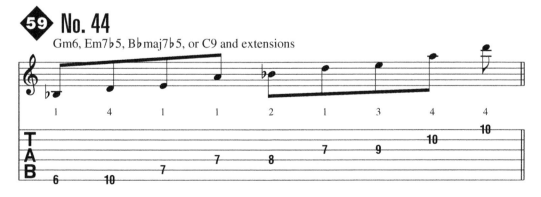

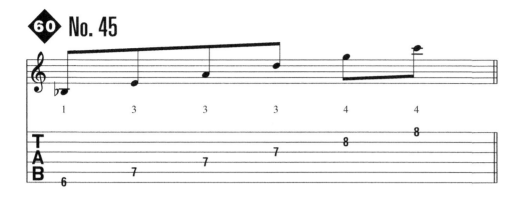

Chord suggestions for these combinations: Gm6, Em7♭5, B♭maj7♭5, or C9 (all extensions and alterations).

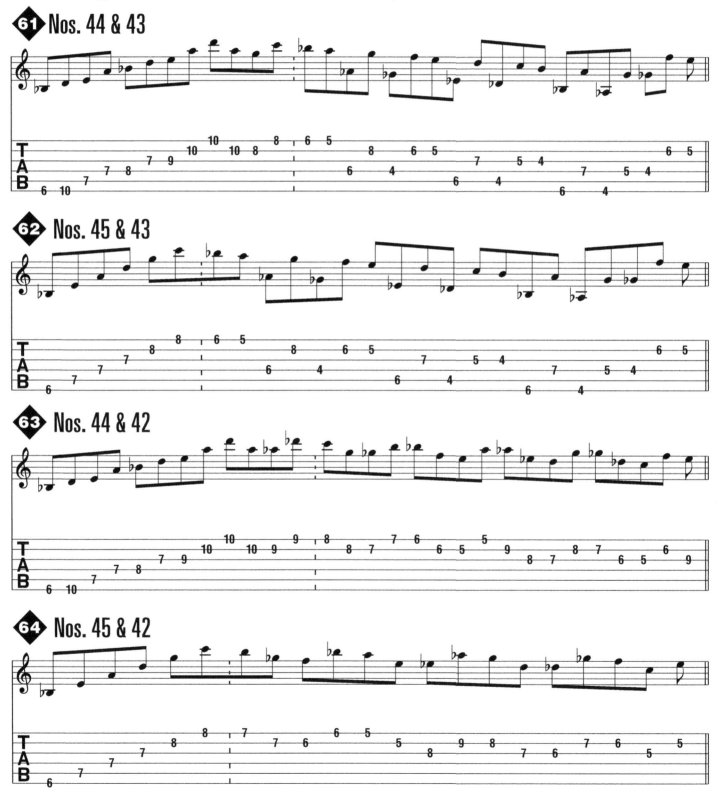

The rest of these designs are not directly related to the chromatic scale but deal with the same chord types.

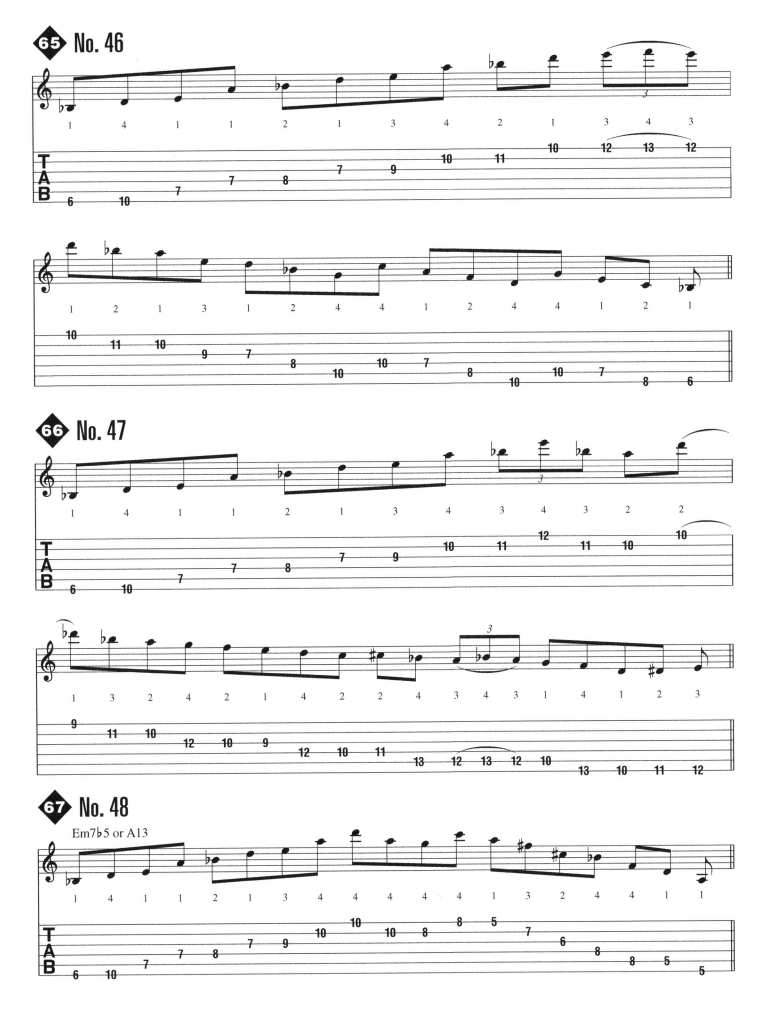

Designs for Conventional Progressions

Here are some four-bar ideas to sound unconventional on the conventional progression of Cmaj7–Am7–Dm7–G7. They also work well for any of the following four-bar sequences. Try designs 49 thru 55 over each of these progressions.

68 No. 49

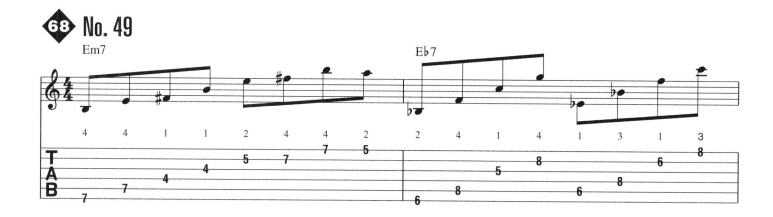

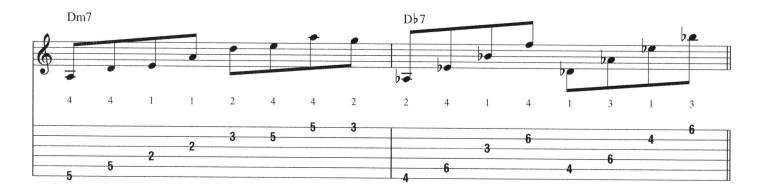

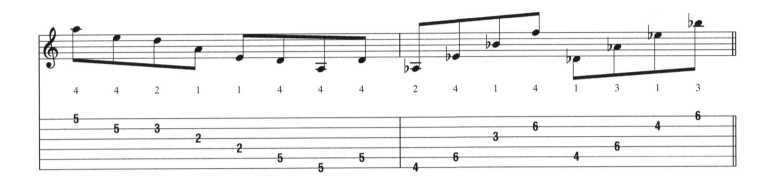

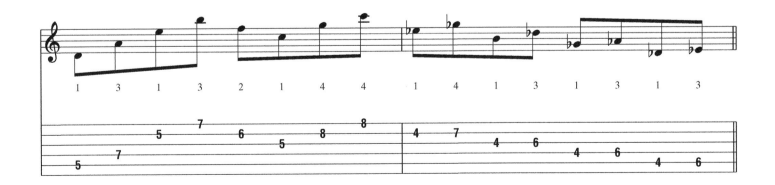

No. 52

No. 53

73 No. 54

74 No. 55

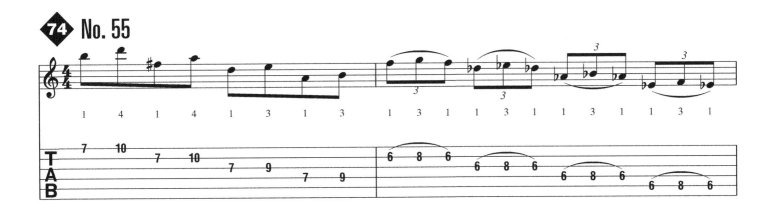

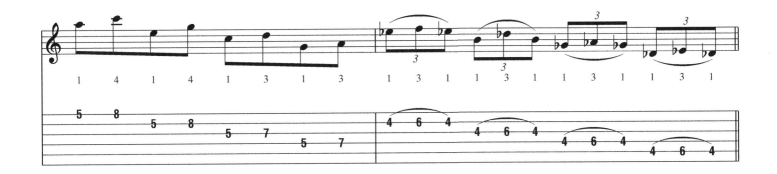

Designs of Varied Harmonic Applications

Designs 56 thru 61 are good examples of how to create tension over one chord (Bm7). The most important thing to remember in outside or atonal playing is to resolve melodically. Notice how we start and end on Bm7. The chords above the music give us a clearer insight into how outside tonality is created. Once these lines are well learned, you will find them popping up in many other musical situations.

No. 56

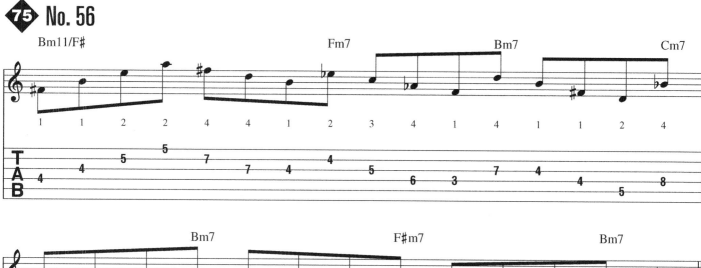

No. 57

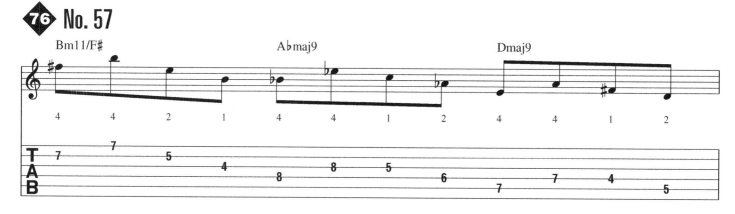

77 No. 58

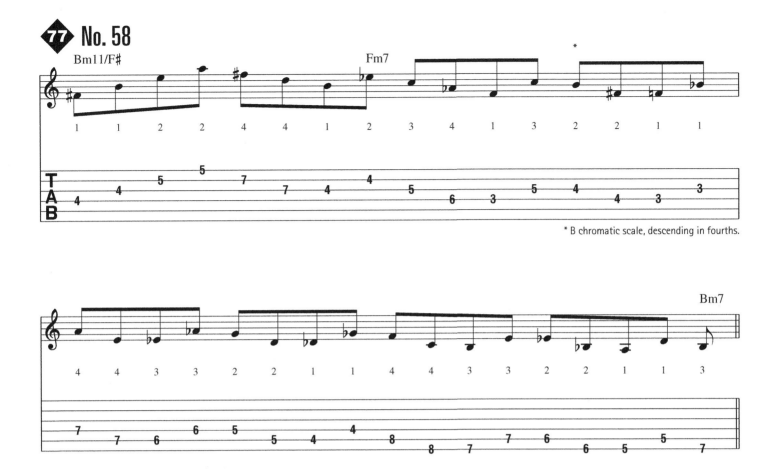

*B chromatic scale, descending in fourths.

Same harmonic structure as no. 56 (no. 59 is no. 56 transposed to the lowest register).

78 No. 59

Same harmony as no. 57 (no. 60 is no. 57 begun in a lower register).

79▶ No. 60

No. 61 is no. 58 in the lowest register.

80▶ No. 61

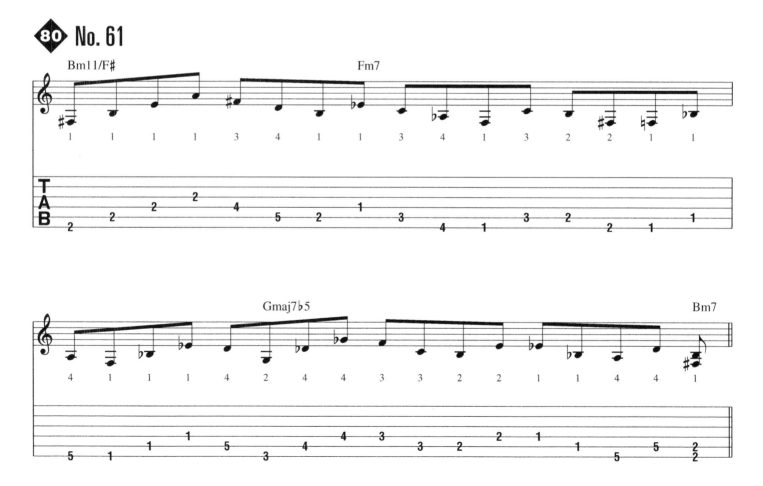

These next two designs work well against Gmaj7♭5 or A13.

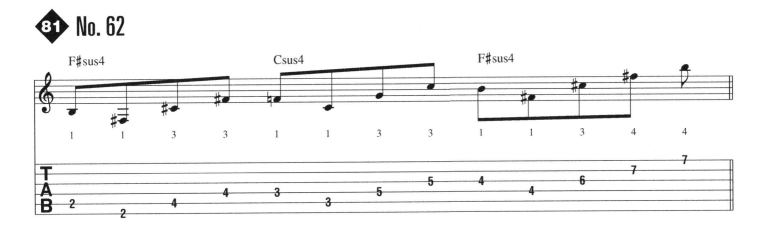

No. 62

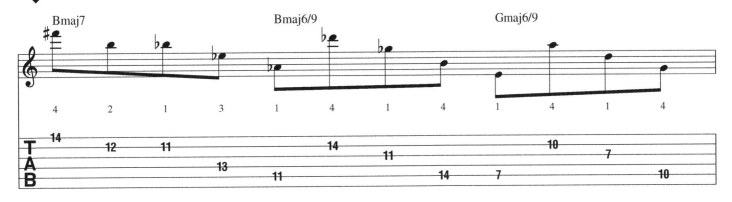

No. 63

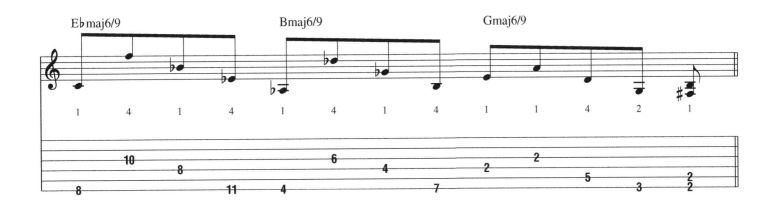

This design is a composite of some of the previous lines.

83 **No. 64**

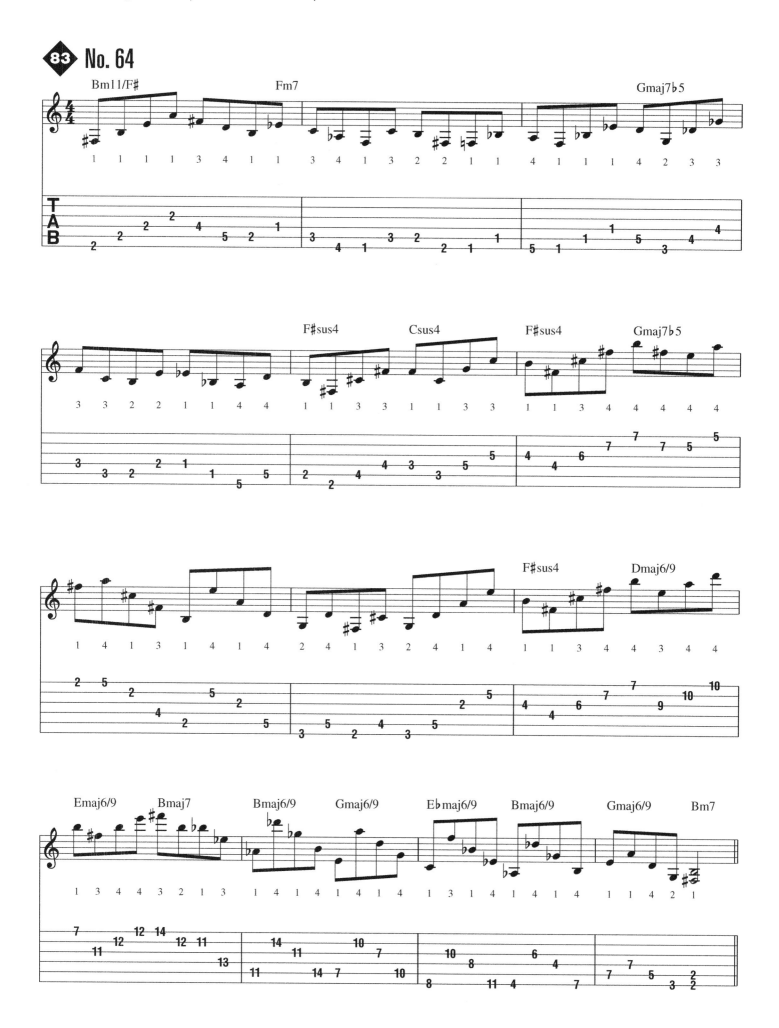

Designs of the Perfect Fifth Interval

Lines 65 thru 70 are built on the perfect fifth interval, progressing up in minor thirds. I have put together several combinations to give you an insight into this very popular interval. You will at once recognize many more possible uses for them. I have found these lines to work well for intros, endings, and freestyle playing.

Note: 65 thru 68 deal with the same four chords placed in different positions. Overall, they convey a Gmaj7 tonality.

88 **No. 69**

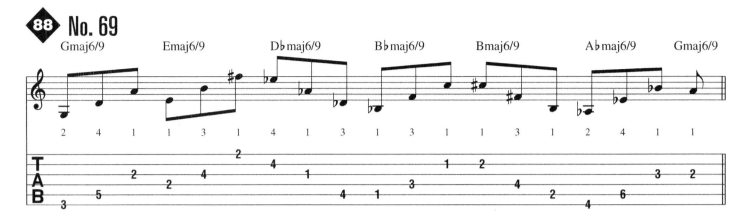

This design has an A♭maj7 tonality.

89 **No. 70**

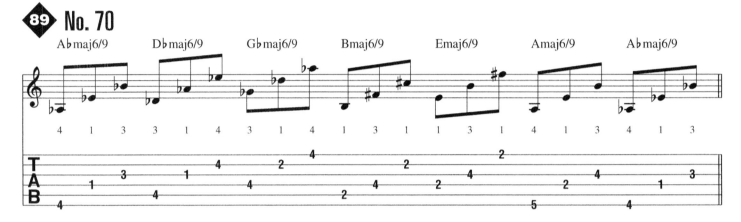

Throughout this book, you will undoubtedly find other chords to fit these lines. For the remainder of this book, I have made very general chord suggestions. Keep stretching your ears; there are many more to be found. This next one works well against D♭m9 or Emaj9.

90 **No. 71**

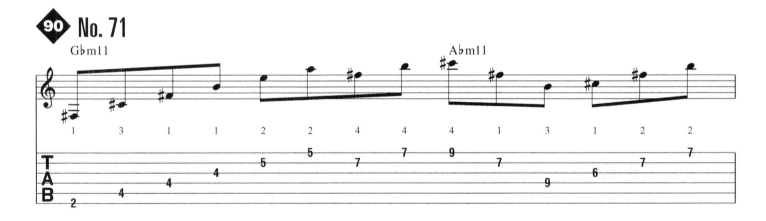

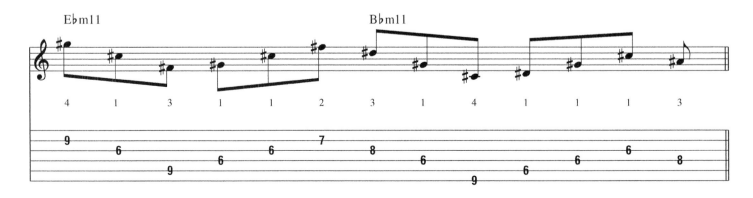

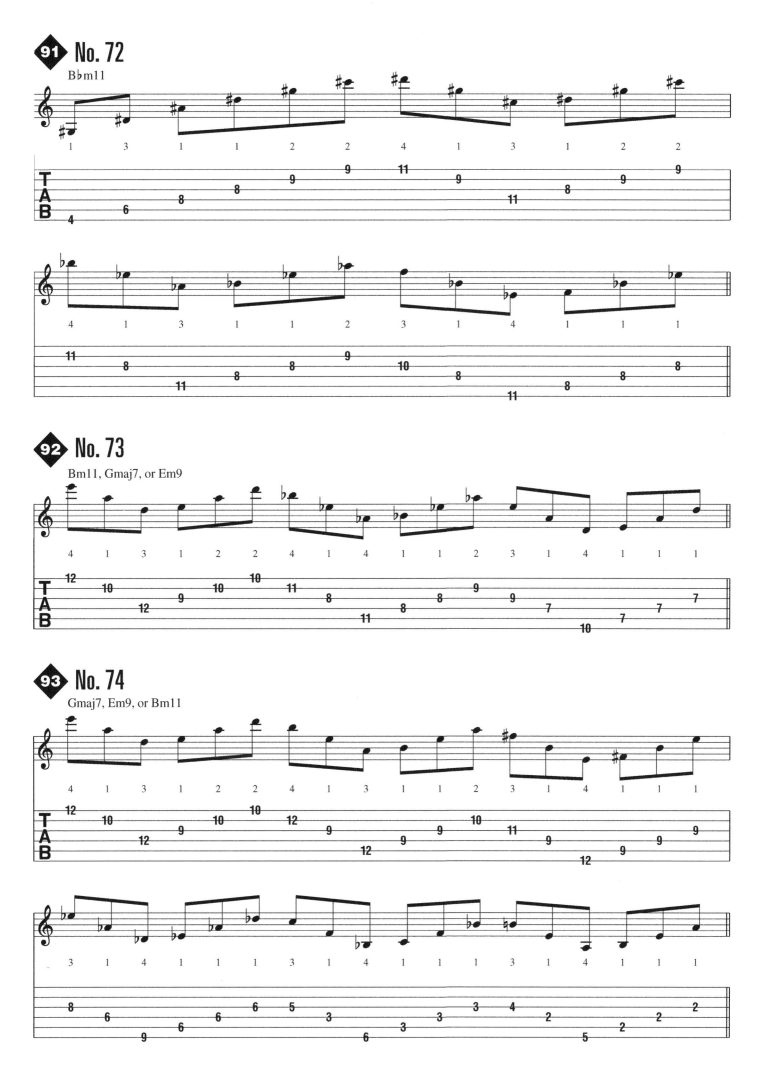

Designs for Freestyle Improvisation

Designs 75 thru 83 are once again in the category of freestyle playing.

94 ◆ No. 75
B♭maj7♭5 or C7♭5♭9

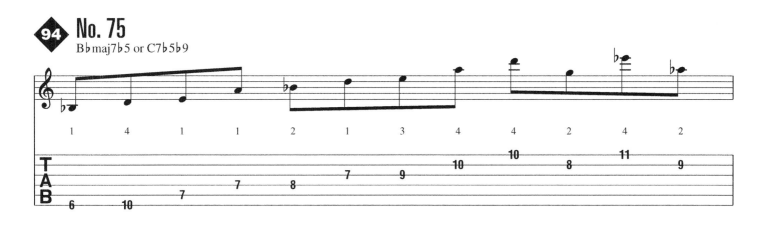

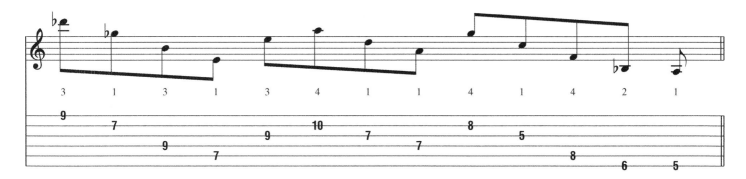

95 ◆ No. 76
F♯m11   Cm11   F♯m11   D♭m11

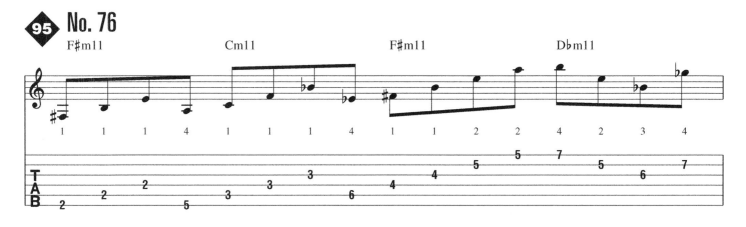

B♭m11   Bm11   B♭m11

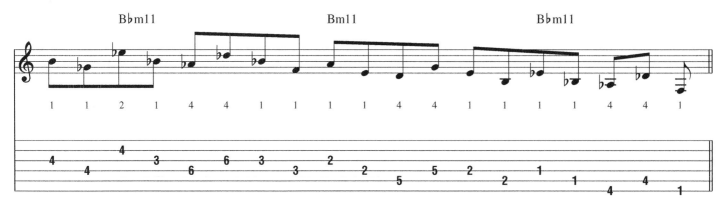

96 # No. 77

B♭maj7♭5 or B♭7 and alterations

97 # No. 78

F♯m11   Fm11   D♭m11   F/A

E♭m11   G♭m11   F/A   E♭m11   G♭m11   Am11

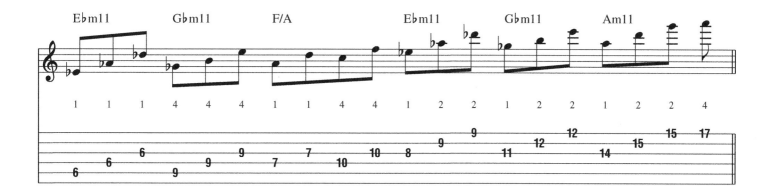

98 # No. 79

Gmaj7♭5 or G7♭5

99 No. 80

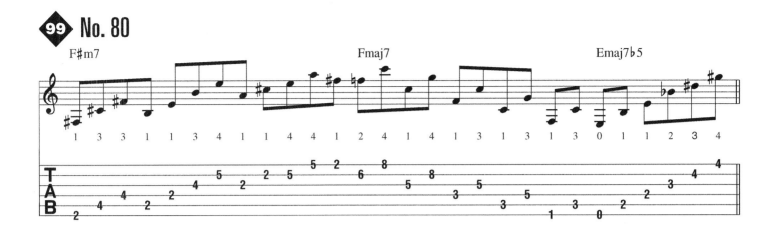

100 No. 81

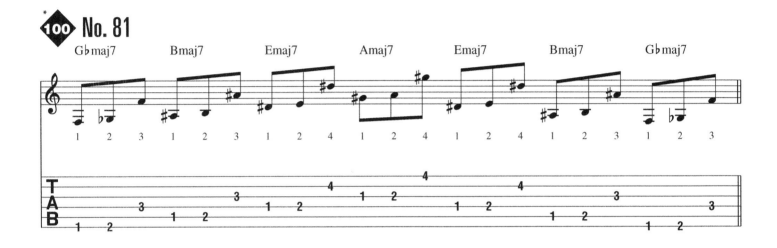

101 No. 82

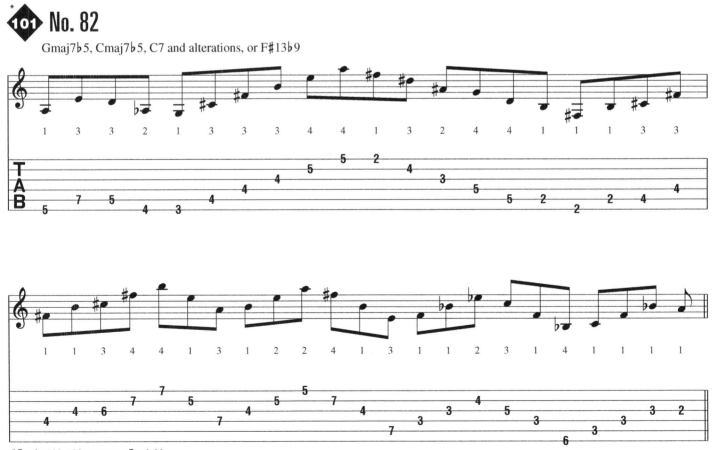

* Tracks 100–102 appear on Track 99

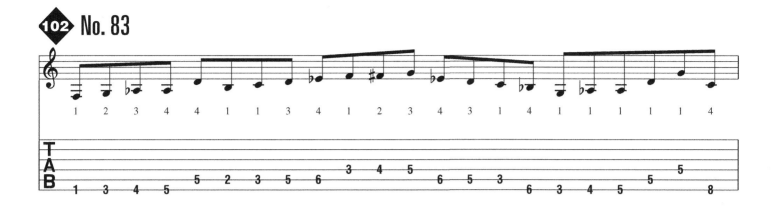

No. 83

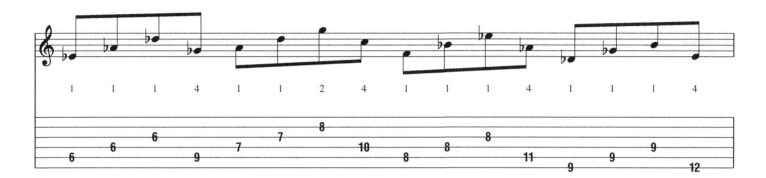

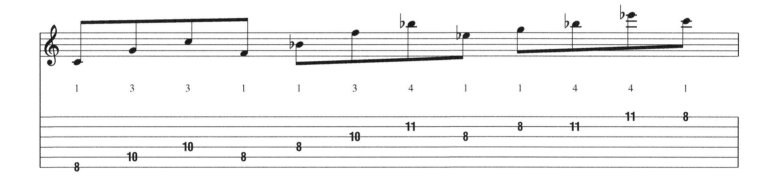

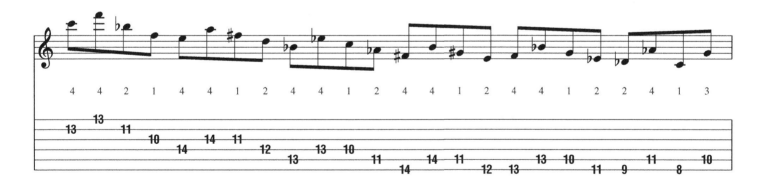

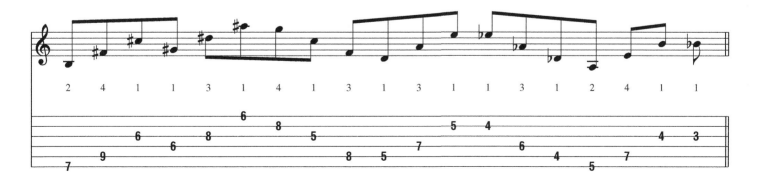

About the Author

With over 30 years experience as a performer and recording artist, Joe Diorio is truly a guitarist's guitarist. He has worked with such jazz luminaries as Sonny Stitt, Eddie Harris, Ira Sullivan, Stan Getz, Horace Silver, and Freddie Hubbard, and his four most recent CD releases include: *I Remember Wes,* a tribute to Wes Montgomery; the solo guitar outing *We Will Meet Again; Double Take,* featuring live performances with bassist Riccardo Del Fra; and *Rare Birds,* a duo album with Mick Goodrick.

Highly respected as an educator, Joe currently teaches at the University of Southern California, Los Angeles, and has conducted jazz guitar seminars throughout the United States, Europe, and Brazil. Additionally, he was one of the three founding instructors for the Guitar Institute of Technology (GIT) in Hollywood, California.

Joe has authored six jazz instructional books and numerous articles for *Guitar Player* magazine, as well as his own instructional video. Visit him on his website at *www.joediorio.com.*

Joe Diorio, ca. 1978

IMPROVE YOUR IMPROV
AND OTHER JAZZ TECHNIQUES WITH BOOKS FROM HAL LEONARD

JAZZ GUITAR

HAL LEONARD GUITAR METHOD
by Jeff Schroedl
The Hal Leonard Jazz Guitar Method is your complete guide to learning jazz guitar. This book uses real jazz songs to teach the basics of accompanying and improvising jazz guitar in the style of Wes Montgomery, Joe Pass, Tal Farlow, Charlie Christian, Pat Martino, Barney Kessel, Jim Hall, and many others.
00695359 Book/Online Audio $22.99

AMAZING PHRASING

50 WAYS TO IMPROVE YOUR
IMPROVISATIONAL SKILLS • *by Tom Kolb*
This book explores all the main components necessary for crafting well-balanced rhythmic and melodic phrases. It also explains how these phrases are put together to form cohesive solos. Many styles are covered – rock, blues, jazz, fusion, country, Latin, funk and more – and all of the concepts are backed up with musical examples.
00695583 Book/Online Audio $22.99

BEST OF JAZZ GUITAR

by Wolf Marshall • Signature Licks
In this book/audio pack, Wolf Marshall provides a hands-on analysis of 10 of the most frequently played tunes in the jazz genre, as played by the leading guitarists of all time. Each selection includes technical analysis and performance notes, biographical sketches, and authentic matching audio with backing tracks.
00695586 Book/Online Audio $29.99

CHORD-MELODY PHRASES FOR GUITAR

by Ron Eschete • REH ProLessons Series
Expand your chord-melody chops with these outstanding jazz phrases! This book covers: chord substitutions, chromatic movements, contrary motion, pedal tones, inner-voice movements, reharmonization techniques, and much more. Includes standard notation and tab, and online audio.
00695628 Book/Online Audio $17.99

CHORDS FOR JAZZ GUITAR

THE COMPLETE GUIDE TO COMPING,
CHORD MELODY AND CHORD SOLOING • *by Charlton Johnson*
This book/audio pack will teach you how to play jazz chords all over the fretboard in a variety of styles and progressions. It covers: voicings, progressions, jazz chord theory, comping, chord melody, chord soloing, voice leading and many more topics. The audio offers 98 full-band demo tracks. No tablature.
00695706 Book/Online Audio $19.99

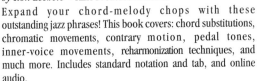

FRETBOARD ROADMAPS – JAZZ GUITAR

THE ESSENTIAL GUITAR PATTERNS
THAT ALL THE PROS KNOW AND USE • *by Fred Sokolow*
This book will get guitarists playing lead & rhythm anywhere on the fretboard, in any key! It teaches a variety of lead guitar styles using moveable patterns, double-note licks, sliding pentatonics and more, through easy-to-follow diagrams and instructions. The online audio includes 54 full-demo tracks.
00695354 Book/Online Audio $17.99

JAZZ IMPROVISATION FOR GUITAR

by Les Wise • REH ProLessons Series
This book/audio will allow you to make the transition from playing disjointed scales and arpeggios to playing melodic jazz solos that maintain continuity and interest for the listener. Topics covered include: tension and resolution, major scale, melodic minor scale, and harmonic minor scale patterns, common licks and substitution techniques, creating altered tension, and more! Features standard notation and tab, and online audio.
00695657 Book/Online Audio $19.99

JAZZ RHYTHM GUITAR
THE COMPLETE GUIDE
by Jack Grassel
This book/audio pack will help rhythm guitarists better understand: chord symbols and voicings, comping styles and patterns, equipment, accessories and set-up, the fingerboard, chord theory, and much more. The accompanying online audio includes 74 full-band tracks.
00695654 Book/Online Audio $24.99

JAZZ SOLOS FOR GUITAR
LEAD GUITAR IN THE STYLES OF TAL FARLOW,
BARNEY KESSEL, WES MONTGOMERY, JOE PASS, JOHNNY SMITH
by Les Wise
Examine the solo concepts of the masters with this book including phrase-by-phrase performance notes, tips on arpeggio substitution, scale substitution, tension and resolution, jazz-blues, chord soloing, and more. The audio includes full demonstration and rhythm-only tracks.
00695447 Book/Online Audio $19.99

100 JAZZ LESSONS
Guitar Lesson Goldmine Series
by John Heussenstamm and Paul Silbergleit
Featuring 100 individual modules covering a giant array of topics, each lesson includes detailed instruction with playing examples presented in standard notation and tablature. You'll also get extremely useful tips, scale diagrams, and more to reinforce your learning experience, plus audio featuring performance demos of all the examples in the book!
00696454 Book/Online Audio $24.99

101 MUST-KNOW JAZZ LICKS

A QUICK, EASY REFERENCE GUIDE
FOR ALL GUITARISTS • *by Wolf Marshall*
Here are 101 definitive licks, plus demonstration audio, from every major jazz guitar style, neatly organized into easy-to-use categories. They're all here: swing and pre-bop, bebop, post-bop modern jazz, hard bop and cool jazz, modal jazz, soul jazz and postmodern jazz. Includes an introduction, tips, and a list of suggested recordings.
00695433 Book/Online Audio $19.99

SWING AND BIG BAND GUITAR

FOUR-TO-THE-BAR COMPING IN THE STYLE OF
FREDDIE GREEN • *by Charlton Johnson*
This unique package teaches the essentials of swing and big band styles, including chord voicings, inversions, substitutions; time and groove, reading charts, chord reduction, and expansion; sample songs, patterns, progressions, and exercises; chord reference library; and online audio with over 50 full-demo examples. Uses chord grids – no tablature.
00695147 Book/Online Audio $22.99

Visit Hal Leonard Online at **www.halleonard.com**

*Prices, contents and availability
subject to change without notice.*